T0114707

I
KNEW
DEEP
DOWN

FARU K. GUDINA

WESTBOW
PRESS®
A DIVISION OF THOMAS NELSON
& ZONDERVAN

WestBow Press books may be ordered through booksellers or by contacting:

WestBow Press
A Division of Thomas Nelson & Zondervan
1663 Liberty Drive
Bloomington, IN 47403
www.westbowpress.com
844-714-3454

ISBN: 978-1-6642-9328-1 (sc)
ISBN: 978-1-6642-9330-4 (hc)
ISBN: 978-1-6642-9329-8 (e)

Library of Congress Control Number: 2023903119

Print information available on the last page.

WestBow Press rev. date: 04/26/2023

Contents

Foreword

My tongue is like the pen of a skillful poet.
Psalm 45:1

I Knew Deep Down is a book of poems written by one of my daughters, Faru K. Gudina. When Faru was in the third grade, a teacher, Mrs. Kidane, saw her potential and called us in for a parent-teacher conference. Her aunt—whom Faru calls Adade—and I went and listened to Faru's first poem, entitled "Day Dreaming," which had only four lines. Faru's aunt and I left the classroom confused, not understanding what the teacher saw in those four lines. We come from a literary culture where poems tell a long story. We could not grasp what the teacher saw in that short poem and left the matter at that.

Faru continued writing and shared the poems from time to time during our family evenings. Her aunt, unlike me, faithfully collected and saved all the poems; little did she know that one day they would be compiled and published as this poetry book.

The poems are reflections of the depth of Faru's thoughts, the sharpness of her observation skills, and the eloquence of her language, which became increasingly pronounced as she grew older. Her ability began to catch the attention of others; at the age of ten, she was selected by her school principal to recite one of her poems to the gathering of female African leaders at the African Union. When Faru read the line "If women are trusted to lead homes, why not countries?" it sent the audience into roaring applause.

As a family, we grew to love and admire the development of her thought. We always marveled at how she condensed and expressed big, deep ideas using only a few words. Her love for nature, expressed

ix

in her childhood poems and paintings, compelled us to think about creation and the Creator of all things, as her sense of humor moved us to laughter, her quest for justice challenged us, and her spiritual fervor inspired us to read more of the scriptures.

The beginning years were all about nature—bees, butterflies, the stars, the moon. When she reached the age of ten, a profound change took over, and social justice became her central theme. Her poem "The Streets of Addis" depicts the harsh conditions homeless children in her home city are exposed to. In "At the Yogurt-Inn," she captures a scene where rich kids indulge in delicacies while poor street kids stand and gaze. Faru possesses a unique ability to capture events and incidents in a profound manner to influence her readers. Reading her poems may bring the reader to laughter or sometimes to tears—or even provoke a person to anger.

Another shift in her thought came when she reached the age of thirteen; for her, a rebellious stage that came along with a lot of questions. The issue of self became her focus: Who am I? Why do I exist? Her poems started to include people around her, questioning teachers and challenging counselors. I see her poem "Madam Psychotherapist" as a genuine representation of the rebellion and consequent havoc teenagers may pose to themselves and their families.

A cross-cutting theme from childhood to adolescence is the subject of faith. Faith, which was handed down to her from two generation of believers, remains central to her thinking and life. Eventually, all of Faru's poems became faith-centric—some are written as dialogs between herself and God. Many of these are yet to be published.

It is my hope that Faru's poems will help young people who are going through life's struggles; set free those who may be captive to misconceptions, unbelief, and all kind of deceptions; and inspire many to put to use their God-given talents. May this book of poetry impart God's love, care for the poor, yearning for justice, and desire for change and transformation to all readers.

Lensa Gudina

Acknowledgments

I vividly remember writing one of my first poems in the third grade. It was in that class I penned my first four-line poem, titled "Day Dreaming." I recall eagerly lining up behind my peers to share it with my teacher, Mrs. Kidane, and her colleague. After I shared my poem, the two teachers exchanged glances without so much as a remark, then stepped aside to let me go to recess. That afternoon, Mrs. Kidane sat me down in private and asked me how and where I got the poem. Confirming that it was written by me seemed to excite her. To my surprise, she went on to book a meeting with my parents–my aunt and mom, as it turned out. Mrs. Kidane's interest was the spark that ignited my journey with poetry.

At home, my aunt and mom always encouraged me by taking time to listen. My poetry readings became a frequent nighttime ritual for the family. I was always insecure about sharing my innermost thoughts. Had it not been for the love and support that God surrounded me with, I would not have had the courage to continue writing.

My little brother, Kolule, not only helped with revising but also was inspired to write a few poems, which he shared anonymously on our family group chat. His poems seemed so similar to mine that I thought I wrote them. To my surprise, my secret admirer, who called himself Albert Meinz, had mastered mimicking my style of writing. Even though Albert Meinz's true identity was eventually disclosed, my brother continues to deny that he has ever written a poem.

My mom continually read and revised my poems, challenging my ideology. Aunt Kullee even bought poetry books in hopes that I would learn from them, despite my lack of discipline to read. Uncle Amitti and our family friend Marti helped by retrieving the dispersed poems and formatting the manuscript. When my parents felt that I had a substantial collection of poems, they shared them with Dr. Samuel Yonas Deressa. He played a crucial role in bringing this poetry book to life by assisting me in publishing and sharing my book with readers.

Throughout my poetic journey, I have received so much support and love from many people, especially those who pray for me. A prime example is my grandmother's prayer group, who still meet at her home for prayer regularly even now that my grandmother has passed. I have been blessed by God with people to carry and support me through prayer and words of encouragement. He surrounded me with an entire army of warriors who continuously prayed over this small gift of mine. May this book be a pleasing aroma to Him.

Bumblebees

Bees always buzzing,
Eager to make honey,
Stinging and hurting people,
Busy to serve the queen.

grade 2
fall 2009

Butterflies

I feel like there are butterflies in my stomach.
I feel like I ate butterflies for breakfast.
I feel like they are rumbling and trying to get free—
I feel like I should let them go free.

grade 2
spring 2009

Kiss

A kiss goodbye is a kiss let go.
A kiss hello is a kiss that will never go!

grade 2
summer 2009

Daydreaming

I am sitting in class, daydreaming.
I see horses racing on the beaches,
all galloping.
I hear birds in the air calling my name
and see the rainbow carrying me away.
I hear snails singing my name: *Faru, Faru, Faru*.
Bees too are buzzing my name.
Finally, the teacher calls my name,
and my dreams fly away.

grade 3
winter 2010

Stars Playing

Flying into the sky up high,
high above the dark clouds
(so tempting to reach at night),
stars are playing high above,
racing one another every night,
pushing anger and darkness so far away—
stars, soaring into the sky up high.

grade 3
summer 2010

Wonderful Sun

The sun is up in the sky,
shining so bright, making everything right,
like billions of stars stuck together,
though it's just one sun; there is no other.
The sun makes my day just right.

grade 3
spring 2010

In My Grandma's Arms

To Mami, Tsehay Tolessa, the best grandma ever

In my grandma's arms I feel safe.
When she holds me, I feel like I could never let go.
I like the way she smiles at me; it makes me feel so loved.
I find pleasure sitting with her
as I watch her voice leave her lips.
I know my grandma won't let me go.
I know for sure she will be there wherever I go.

grade 3
winter 2010

Raindrops

Raindrops are much like teardrops.
When it rains,
it's like the angels are crying.
Every drop is special
because it is raining.

grade 3
spring 2010

Is It Me or the Moon?

Looking in the mirror,
my complexion is gold—
or perhaps the color of cheese?
Oh, look! This side of mine is so bright,
but my other side is so dark.
Is that a pimple I spot, or a beauty mole?
I am a vision that people wish to see.
I have no doubt that you dream of me.
You might want to touch me, for I am the moon.
But I can only be seen from far and admired,
Never to be touched nor disturbed.

grade 4
spring 2011

Tiger Sunset

Sinking below the mountain,
a tiger-orange sunset
beams and smiles as it declares the day's end.
It descends so low, only to rise on the other side.

grade 4
spring 2011

Just a Wish

A wish to the heavens,
a wish that hope never dies,
that faith never withers,
that love no more flees;
a wish sent up to the skies
for laughter to fill this barren air,
a wish to God,
a wish for water,
for dew from heaven,
springs from below—
A wish to refresh and grow …

grade 5
spring 2012

Adade and Lelo: Two Sides of a Coin

My aunt and my mom are so close,
twisted together like a rope,
two sides of a coin no one can separate.
They work together, pray together,
drive, eat, dream, and plan together.
One thing impossible to split in the world
is my aunt and my mom.
After all, they are two sides of a coin,
woven together so tight;
nothing can separate
my aunt and my mom.

grade 5
summer 2012

Whom to Talk To

Talk to the wind;
dialogue with the animals.

Whisper to the leaves;
smile at the sun.

Kneel down to murmur to the insects;
hum to the birds;
buzz to the bees;
speak to those who can't speak;
voice the silence of the voiceless!

grade 5
spring 2012

The Moon

It goes around, the moon.
The moon is so bright.
It comes up some nights,
Making my face light up.
Then it hides behind the clouds.
Will it ever come back?
It breaks my little heart. The moon!
It emerges again, smiling at me.
The moon, so beautiful—
It shines so bright
With all its might.
Oh, how I love to watch the moon!

grade 5
winter 2012

That Monster

So big, so huge,
so bad, so mean,
stronger than a rock,
harder than a wall,
it strikes the big;
it hurts the small.
It shakes your base and breaks your heart.
It makes me sad; it makes me cry,
that monster called poverty!

grade 5
summer 2012

Just Like You, Wedu

To my sister

I always wanted to be just like you.
I wanted to dress, eat, and sleep like you.
I wanted to walk like you, talk like you.
I wanted to be smart like you, focused just like you.
I wanted to be just like you.
I wanted to act like you.
But more than wanting to be like you, I wanted to be near you.
I wanted you to be the person I could lean on,
share my pains and endless concerns.
I wanted to cry on your shoulder.
I wanted to draw closer,
but time seemed dearer to you.
You left no time, no space for me to draw nearer.
All I wanted was to be just like you,
draw a little closer to you,
Wedu, just like you!

grade 6
summer 2013

Next

Next in line
to hear a cheer,
next in line
to get a job,
next in line
to pay the bills,
next in line
all the time,
next in line
to be on the top—
next in line to get into a new line …

grade 6
fall 2013

A Star

A star in the night,
a twinkle in the dark,
sparkling from above,
shimmering and glittering—
I wonder what your true color is:
red, blue, or yellow?
I really don't know.
But I know you are there,
shining in the dark,
pushing away the dusky gloom,
sparkling through the long night,
glimmering and flickering,
ushering in the long-awaited hope,
oh, little sparkling and glittery star!

grade 6
winter 2013

A Step

I step a step.
I step toward the future,
a step away from the past.

I step to the rain,
a step further from drought.
I step toward farming,
a step away from hunger.

I step to laughter,
a step away from tears.
I step toward kindness,
a step away from poverty.

I step to a better world—
a step I want to take with you.

grade 6
winter 2013

The Streets of Addis

Streets strewn full of beggars
begging for scraps and coins,
beggars of all ages,
infants in women's arms,
orphans sleeping on side roads,
the elderly stretching out their arms,
all pleading for leftovers:

the privileged walk past without looking.
As beggars persist for a meal,
the privileged unmindfully gobble more food.
As the beggars grow thin and frail,
the privileged enlarge and expand.

Tears run down my cheeks,
for there is so much to do
yet little time and power.

grade 6
summer 2013

A Seed

A seed is so small, so trivial, so insignificant,
easy to lose, easy to crush.
Who'd ever imagine that one day it will be so big?
No longer a seed but a vast tree,
a shade to humanity and beasts alike,
much like a child who was once weak,
so frail and fragile in unknown hands.
No one ponders that one day it will grow,
develop, and transform like that single seed:
no longer a delicate child, stranded without help,
but full-grown and mature,
guiding and supporting,
leading and transforming.
Today's seed, today's child;
tomorrow's shade, tomorrow's hope.

grade 7
spring 2014

Age

As I grow older, I see strange things appear.
Age makes me despair.
As I count my years, I hear my voice grow louder and louder.
Will people hear what I have to say?
As I blow out my birthday candles, I hear my heart pounding.
Could my lungs be failing me, cutting short my breath?
As I skim through my photos, I see my pictures fade.
Oh, my memories, will they disintegrate?
How much I hate aging, for it is the path to the end,
fading away beauty and sapping vigor and strength,
bringing me to a place of no remembrance,
spreading its shadows over the marks I bear.
"No," I say; I push the glooms away,
for when I wake up tomorrow, I will have a brighter day.
When I get to heaven someday, I will neither age nor decay.

grade 7
fall 2014

Evil Spirit

Evil spirit, evil wishes,
I cast you off, away from me!
Evil thoughts, evil views,
I give you over to hell, for that's where you belong.
Evil spirit, evil words,
I toss you to the ends of the earth!
Evil spirts, evil schemes, you cannot lure me!
I resist you; you have no power over me.
Evil spirit, you cannot draw near me,
for I have that precious almighty blood on me.

grade 7
summer 2014

Superhero

To my loving auntie, Adade, friend of the poor,
my hero who keeps me safe and inspired

She cannot fly like Superman;
no might in sight, no strength, nothing like the Hulk.
She has no speed like the lightning Flash,
no blazing rapidity,
nothing that our generation admires nor desires,
no flying cape like Wonder Woman nor spider webs like Spider-Man.

What she has is as rare as diamond
you can neither buy nor swap.
A golden heart she has,
incomparable kindness,
unconditionally generous.
She is one at heart,
a friend to the poor and the powerless,
not a superhero but super generous,
and nothing can stop her in loving the helpless.

grade 8
winter 2014

Forgive and Forget

To souls I might have caused pain

Pleading for mercy, here I stand
asking for forgiveness,
regretting my negligence,
lamenting over my ignorance,
the pain I might have caused,
the agony of my indifference.

Your tearful eyes,
your broken heart,
fragmented spirit,
shattered emotions—
I pray that you forgive me.
I hope that you forget
the hurt I caused,
the pain I inflicted.

I write with tears
Pouring out my heart's contents.
I never intended any harm
nor envisioned damage—
sheer negligence,
utter ignorance!
My sincere apologies,
genuine confessions.

Allow me to say I care.
I do share the pain.
Please forgive and forget;
let love lead.

grade 8
winter 2014

I Look for You

I look for you.
My head turns left and right.
I call on you all night.
I whisper your name and scream it out loud:
"Jesus, come and help me now!"
I search for signs you might have left behind.
I open doors and hope to find you inside.
I look high and low, but you are nowhere in sight,
so I sit down in frustration. As tears blur my eyes,
I feel a hand on my shoulder, so assuring.
I look up and see you come and hug me tight.
I see your face and realize you have been with me all along
my ever-present help—Jesus!

grade 7
summer 2014

God-Given Identity

Look how I walk with pride!
You can see from my strides
no trace of shame on me.
Just look at how my head is held up high.

Enlightened and sophisticated,
notice how eloquently I speak.

I am proud of who I am, my God-given identity,
for I come from a nation that is rich and wide,
where beauty and elegance abound.

grade 7
summer 2014

Merciless Past

I open my eyes
only to wish to close them.
I feel out of time and place,
wishing I could go back to the past decade.
I cry, moan, sob, and say "What if I could fly?"
I would take no glimpse of the past—
the past, a merciless reminder of tears and groans,
a cruel souvenir of broken families,
a cue to crumbling trust and family values,
flashbacks of bloodshed
under the guise of religion and culture.
I refuse to look back and face the reality of today.
I would rather close my eyes and simply fly away.

grade 8
fall 2014

Rape

To defenseless rape victims

I am a girl, a woman,
a human being just like you,
created in God's image and likeness.
I have dreams and aspirations,
boundless hopes and desires,
rivers I wish to cross, mountains I hope to climb.
I've plans to make and goals to reach, unlike you.
I thirst to learn; I dream to grow,
long to excel, desire to achieve,
build a home and make a family.

But you chose force, utter coercion,
robing me of my purity, depriving my sanity.
You spoiled an act intended to be sacred.
You trampled over my humanity.
You crushed my dreams, trod on my aspirations.
You shook my faith and overshadowed my hope.
You made me slip and fall,
brought me shame, total disgrace.
Your indecent, vulgar steps
incite rage in me, provoking me to anger,
inflaming vengefulness, unknown viciousness.
You've taught the innocent spitefulness,
rubbed your endless malice on me.

At the sight of you I scowl;
hearing your name, I frown.
But if I expose what you have done,
would I be heard and granted justice?
Or would my case be mocked and overlooked?
Shall I leave it to my God,
His divine and righteous judgment?
For when you touched me, He saw and scowled.
His smile faded, and He frowned.
When you touched me, the angels cried,
for you broke God's law,
trampling me down with no mercy.
But God has picked me up.
You dusted my dreams,
but my God has strengthened me,
deploying his mighty angels on my path.

So next time you try to touch,
next time you step near,
His wrath will be unleashed
to pay into your evil laps the due penalty you deserve.

grade 7
fall 2014

O Lord, Rescue Me

Lord, I have been chained and shackled by my enemies.
O Lord, rescue me;
do not let me be put to shame,
open wounds, salt grinded in between.
O Lord, rescue me;
do not let me be disgraced.
My reputation has been dragged in the
dirt alongside my family name.
O Lord, rescue me;
do not let me be put to shame.
I have been shunned and thrown out the gates.
O My Comfort, my hope,
do not let me be put to indignity,
for without your mercy, I am to blame.
Mercy! Have mercy on me!

grade 7
summer 2014

Think and Consider

Think about the leaves and the trees.
Tick tock, think.
Think about your failures and success stories.
Tick tock, think.
Think about your future and history.
Tick tock, think.
Think about all your pain and misery.
Tick tock, think.
Think about your regrets and repents.
Tick tock, think.
Think about your time that is running out.
Tick tock, think.

grade 7
summer 2014

Friends

Friends forever.
How long is forever?
Is it as big as our hugs,
or as loud as our laughs?
Is it as long as our adventures together,
or as expensive as our long phone conversations?

Best friends.
What makes us the best?
Is it the way we try to look identical,
or how we tell each other secrets?
Is it the times we had together,
Or how hard we cried when we were apart?

Friends till the very end.
But when is the end?
Is it when you tell all my secrets,
or when I cry?
Is it when I find a new one,
Or when I die?

Friends.
Does it have to come to an end?

grade 7
fall 2014

Yogurt-Inn in Addis

Yogurt-Inn is for the rich and indulging,
for those with full tummies but ever wanting more
exotic flavors, delightful aromas.
Every mouthful could be savored—
but not by the children across the street,
shivering in the cold, staring without ceasing
at scoops of frozen yogurt right in front of me,
amaretto, vanilla, chocolate, and caramel,
syrup dripping, crunchy granola, raisins of sorts.
Exuberance! Aroma, texture, and color!
Time for delight and joy!

A glimpse at the street children turns the sweet taste sour,
every spoonful tasting more and more bitter,
every flavor stinging like a bee,
every swallow going down like a bullet,
turning my stomach sour.
Children of my age with no parents to look after them;
no charities, no churches, no governments to care.
I detest the food, the place, and everything else.
I grab my yogurt cup and strode towards a begging child,
so humbled I felt I could do that,
excited about the joy I was going to bring,
dreaming of the orphanages that I will one day build.

A guard with a club in his hand emerges out of the dark,
smashing the poor kid to the ground
nowhere to be found ever again.
Now it was my turn to cry bitterly,
not understanding the aimless cruelty
that evening at the Yogurt-Inn.

grade 7
summer 2014

A Tribute to Mami

To my grandma, a hero of faith

A path of suffering my grandma chose to walk,
the kind of path Christ Himself chose to trudge.
When Grandpa Gudina was stuck at the crossroad,
wondering why he was created and what God wanted
(is it to be a doctor or a pastor? utterly confused),
full of wisdom and insights my grandma exclaimed,
"Why become a doctor and limit yourself to treat mere flesh?
Go holistic, be a pastor! God created man—body, spirit, and soul."
She knew she was opting for a rougher, narrower path,
a path that would demand her dear husband's life.
If she had only opted for an easier path,
she'd have spared herself ten years of confinement,
saved herself from wounds and scars of torture.
She certainly would have avoided the constant threat of murder.
I always nagged, "Why, Mami, why did you choose to suffer?"
"I have to carry the wounds of Christ" was her constant answer.
Opting to have a church in her compound;
opening her doors all year round
to the homeless, the mentally ill, young and old alike;
putting her personal safety and property on the line—
her choice to carry Christ's wounds on her body bore much fruit.
It paved the way for hundreds and thousands
in darkness to see the Light.

Yes, she is to be remembered as a hero of faith,
but what should we do with the legacy she left?
Shouldn't we also opt for the path of self-sacrifice to benefit others?
Do we dare to carry on our bodies the wounds of Christ as Mami did?

grade 7
fall 2014

No More ... but More

No more tears,
But more of laughter.
No more lies,
But more of the truth.
No more failures,
But more accomplishments.

No more hate,
But more of love.
No more killing,
But more of saving.
No more betrayal,
But more of loyalty.
No more negligence,
But more of caring.
No more isolation,
But more of embracing.

No more discord,
But more of harmony.
No more depriving,
But more of sharing.
No more, no more!

grade 8
winter 2015

A Mystified Teenager

My name feels meaningless,
my age pointless.
Everything about me is like thin air,
hard to see, hard to comprehend.
My personality reaches as far as the stars—
unreachable, unpredictable.
My dreams, as numerous as sand on the beach,
are impossible to count or proclaim.
My morals and methods are hazy and foggy,
Unclear, blurred and heavy with mist.
I am like a puzzle hard to fathom,
like a riddle stunning the wise.
If you could only put my pieces back together,
you would understand me better,
for I am a mystified teenager.

grade 8
fall 2015

My Refuge

On the path of life, I stumble, I fall, I bleed.
I look around in search for sympathy:
no friend, no family, no relatives to help.
I agonize and shed bitter tears;
I cry and sob in fear of death.
Lost and lonesome, no family to count on,
isolated on a cold and gloomy island …
what's there to live for? No dreams, no aspirations,
no family, no friends—
I'm just a forlorn, desperate orphan.
I look up towards heaven, beyond the dark clouds,
farther than the gloomy skies.
The rays of hope flicker at me.
I hear myself mumbling, "My God, my light,
my shelter, my hiding place, my refuge.
You are always with me, ever present."
As I enter into your presence, your love surrounds me.
I gaze at your holiness and beauty.
My hope, my joy, my refuge
stood by me when no one would.
Be my refuge, my home, my hiding place—my God.

grade 8
fall 2015

Anger

I fight the voice that urges me to yell, scream, brawl, and broil.
I resist saying, "No more, just go away!"
I try to push that forceful voice,
but it persists to plunge me into the pool of anger.
I gather my strength and struggle to drive the feeling out,
yet it seems to be winning.
I turn around and throw a punch—
I feel like I might even win,
but it gets a hold of me again,
this time harder and faster.
It drags me away to unknown places.
Tears stream down my face.
No, I don't want to be angry or bitter,
nor do I want to hate or hurt.
In a blink of an eye comes my Savior, my Deliverer.
I cry and ask Him to take over my emotions;
I plead with Him to stop this pain.
His kind and trustworthy eyes tell me everything will be all right.
Anger gives way to peace; joy takes over.
Ranting and raving surrender to calmness and tranquility.
I lean back and watch dark thoughts vanish,
for my Savior is my Knight.
He is my Sword and my Shield.
My Liberator always stands by my side,
Ever present in times of need.

grade 8
spring 2015

I Knew Deep Down

To my loving auntie, Adade

As I came to life and took my very first breath,
I knew deep down …

As I took my first bath and enjoyed the warmth of the water,
I knew deep down …

As I opened my eyes and saw the daylight,
I knew deep down …

As I stuttered my first word and let my cry out,
I knew deep down …

I have always known, deep down:
I was put on this earth to feed the hungry,
clothe the naked, shelter the homeless,
and love the lonely.
I was born that way,
created to help the destitute,
to uphold the cause of the poor,
and as I write this, I know deep down
that you were born for that purpose too!

grade 8
summer 2015

A Little Thing Called Faith

You ask me how I know there is a God up there.
You exclaim, "He is not visible nor touchable!"
I raise my eyebrow and ask back,
"How do you know that there is wind?
After all, wind has never shown its face."

You complain and contest when I read the Bible.
You argue, "How do you know it's true or current?"
I smile and whisper, "How do you know
that you need oxygen to breathe?"
I laugh and add, "How come you don't forget to inhale and exhale?"

You get irritated and blurt, "What makes your
God better than other beings?"
I sigh for a moment and begin to speak:
"Faith enabled me to see Him and touch Him.
I saw Him in times of loneliness
right there beside me, amidst darkness,
comforting me with His gentle words—
words of truth I read in the Bible,
which held me up and sustained me.
I know this for sure, not by ignorance
but because of little thing called faith."

grade 8
spring 2015

Part and Parcel of History

History, so ancient, so deep,
standing still, glaring at the passing
mocking centuries, looking down on eras:

nations fight to make history;
heroes die to grab their spot.
History, made of blood and tears,
glimpses of yellow daisies and cheers,
full of discoveries and downfalls—
am I also part and parcel?
Has it made me a fragment, like a brick in the wall?
Without a brick, the wall would be smaller.
Deprived of me, history will be lesser;
never would history be willing to let me depart.

grade 8
fall 2015

Madam Psychotherapist

I sit here and wonder when you will finish your endless talk.
I bite my tongue so I won't erupt.
I fight the urge inside me to walk out.
I look up at the light,
terrified that eye contact with you might make me burn out.
Well-mannered as I am, I know that it's not right to
turn my back on you when you talk.
So I will sit here and listen as you endlessly talk,
and I solemnly promise not to mock.
For I perceive that you adore to talk,
so when my time comes to talk
vow to me that you won't block my dialog.

grade 8
winter 2015

That One Night

When tears of joy wash down your face,
when laughter and delight fill the air,
when angels burst into holy singing from heavens high above,
when darkness hastens out the back door,
when heavenly lights conquer the whole creation,
when a new beginning pushes forth,
when flickers of hope drop everywhere—
That one night
Is when Christ was born.

grade 8
winter 2015

Reason To Hate?

There is a reason to breathe,
a reason to be silent,
a reason to live,
a reason to die,
a reason to laugh,
a reason to cry,
a reason to fall
and a reason to rise,
a reason to love—
but there is no reason to hate.

grade 8
spring 2015

Seasons

When winter vanishes and spring arrives,
when ice breaks and rivers ramble,
when warmth strolls in and cold rushes out,
when birds chant and people savor,
when new life commences, it makes me teem with joy.

grade 8
spring 2015

Suicide

Wicked contemplation crowds my mind;
evil considerations press my soul.
What if I take my life now? If I try to stop my breath,
what will happen?
Not to me, not to my legacy, but rather to my family—
will my mom's heart break or simply stop?
Will my father shed tears or be angry with me?
Will my siblings wish to join me, or will they laugh out loud?
Will my friends mourn, or will they forget all the good times?
Would family and friends care whether they miss me or not?

I know for sure the angels in the sky will weep.
My Father in heaven will frown and shake his head.
Destroying life which never belonged to me,
tampering with God's designs and plans—
who could bear the consequence?
Eternal agony, infinite punishment,
for only God knows that I could have
changed the world if I had tried.
Had I hung onto my life, I could have helped others in the dark.
Only God knows who I could have become,
but I gave up too early to find out.

No!
I should push away such futile thoughts, gloomy and dark,
dragging me down to the murky, slimy valley of the shadow of death.
I will firmly hold on to today and march towards tomorrow,
for I want to see what God has planned for me—
plans to prosper me, not to harm me,
plans to give me a future, overflowing with hope and eternal joy!

grade 8
winter 2015

Sidestep or Charge?

Sidestep failure,
charge at success.
Sidestep weakness,
charge with all your strength.
Sidestep sadness,
charge towards joy.
Sidestep and charge!

grade 8
summer 2015

Let Our Children Go

We march in protest. Our voices scream:
Let our children go and the world know!

Our blood spills, flowing like a stream.
Let our children go and the world know!

Our men have been captured:
no more ecstasy, no more rapture.
Let our children go and the world know!

Our women have been warned not to shed tears,
to show neither remorse nor slight sorrow
over dead bodies, instant orphans.
Let our children go and the world know!

Our girls have been raped and ripped,
their childhood stolen, shredded dreams,
Robbed of dignity, trodden identity.
Let our children go and the world know!

We cry out loud. Won't the world hear
our outcry for mercy, our songs of agony?
Let our children go and the world know!

grade 8
fall 2015

An Urge to Retaliate

A bowl full of fury rages in me.
Tears of anger wash my face.
My mouth is brimming with words of hate.
I have a fistful of regrets
and no space for repentance.

I have a thought of sin overpowering me
with a devilish smile and a leering look;
an urge to retaliate, an impulse to hit,
desire to brawl, on the verge to strike—
my mind is blinded,
insanity looming over me.

I take a deep breath as I stroll away from the scene,
conscience awakened, senses stirred.
Reasoning steps in; self-control sets in.
Why am I so furious, why so embittered?
It's not worth my time nor worth my future.
Away from me, fury! Be far from me, bitterness!
Let me forgive, forget, and restore peace.

grade 8
winter 2015

Fear

Fear of being ugly?
Fear not! You are beautiful.
Fear of the dark?
Fear not! Your Light has come.
Fear of failing?
Fear not! For you shall rise.
Fear of fear?
Fear not! For fear has been overcome.

grade 8
spring 2015

Too Soon, Too Late

Too soon to say hello,
too late to say goodbye;
too soon to inhale,
too late to exhale.
Are you too soon to judge me from the outside?
Too late to look at me from the inside.
Too soon to be too late;
too late to be too soon.

grade 8
summer 2015

Airport Madness

Mombasa Airport, 2016

Congested runways, crowded hallways
teeming with people of all races,
all racing, arriving but departing,
dragging luggage, searching for gates,
dreading inevitable security checks;

weary and squinty eyes,
messy hair, wrinkled shirts;
long toilet lines;
cranky children, worn out parents;
constant mumbles and murmurs in all languages,
eye-catching costumes, exotic faces
bringing memories of UN summits;

no moment of silence, no peace of mind;
constant announcements, endless advertisements
crowding the mind, stealing our thoughts;
occupied seats, slumbering bodies:

airports, ever crowded, swarming with nations
always taking me to new heights and new destinations.

grade 9

Bring Back Freedom

Once upon a time,
back in the olden days,
a proud nation with abundant members,
abounded with peace and strength,
our land extending from north to south.
Our women once had faces that were works of art,
voices that chimed in our heads,
telling us to stand tall and fight back.
Our men, with the strength of ten cows each,
fought bravely when things weren't right.
Our children ran fast and far, contained
knowledge beyond their years.
Oh, why are not our women's voices no longer chiming?
Why were they shushed and put to silence?
Our men could no longer fight back,
for they were shot and buried in graves unmarked.
We stand and watch our land being ripped to shreds;
why can't we regain our strength?
Bring back the olden days when children ran and played,
When the women spoke up and never shied away,
where our men defended and defeated,
that we may stand tall and roam freely in our homeland.

grade 9
Fall 2016

58

Those Hands

My eyes dart from here to there.
I don't want them to catch me today.
Those hands … those devious hands:
I once used them to help me get up;
now they want to push me into a dump,
deep into the pit, down far below,
where I only hear my own echo.
Those same hands that once gave me directions
are now digging my grave.
"Down you go," they say.
Unflinching, I resolve; I turn around and decide
those hands, those wicked hands, won't grasp me today.
I tell myself, "I hate those disgraceful, scandalous hands.
I should get rid of them today!"
All of a sudden it dawns on me: it's not the hands doing the evil,
rather powers that snuck into my thoughts,
urging my hands to tear and destroy, to steal and kill.
Shouldn't I be facing the destroyer behind this,
and not harmless hands created to do good works?
How many times do we target the innocent
in countless wrong battles we choose to fight?
Please make me a strategic warrior who knows her enemies.

grade 9
summer 2016

59

Aspirations

To the children of the diaspora

How long will I have to wait?
How long will I have to pace?
How long till I feel freedom in my veins?
When will I be able to stroll free without fear and terror?
When will I see my sisters and brothers,
Share in their dreams and pains?
How long till we have equal opportunities?
Which way do I go?
Which hour will it be when I see my dreams come true?
When can I finally be me?
How long before I can feel as free as a child can be
In my beautiful country, my home and motherland?

grade 9
Spring 2016

You Are There with Me

I look for you.
I turn left and right.
I call on you all night.
I whisper your name and scream it out loud.
I say, "Jesus—the Source of life!
Reveal yourself to me—the Spring of true love."
I look for signs you might have left behind.
I open doors and hope to find you inside.
I look high and low, but you are nowhere in sight.
I sit down, and when I'm about to cry,
you emerge and lift me high,
higher than the mountains, way above the clouds.
I gaze in your face and realize that you were with me all along.

grade 9
spring 2016

Stop

Stop it!
Stop the bleeding, the lost bodies, and tinted memories.

Stop it!
Stop the looks of confusion, distrust, and grief
that live side by side, full of hate and suspicion.

Stop it!
Stop hate, discrimination, advocating separation.
How did we meet? What placed us side by side?
Can't we agree that God made us all equally?

Stop it!
Let's stop the killing,
the gruesome bombing;
scheming discrimination,
hurling multilateral derogatory terms.

Can we agree to STOP loathing one another?
Stop that cancerous monster called hatred
before it gobbles up our future,
for it shall render us cursed and barren.

grade 9
fall 2016

Sellout

Snitch, rat, traitor:
our mothers mourn because of your greed.
Betrayer, deserter, double agent,
you sold our people for personal comfort.
Opportunist, money-lover, fortune-hunter,
oh, how I loathe and abhor your conduct.
I mourn for you because you are depraved at heart,
alien to principles, no trace of morals, devoid of faith!
Selling the innocent for a handful of coins,
breaking up families, multiplying orphans,
justifying your actions on false premises,
you deceive yourself saying,
"I'm just caring for my family, fending for my children,"
when all you care about is collecting blood-stained coins.
Remember, tomorrow will be different;
no traitor in history ever remained concealed.
If you don't stop, you will meet Judas's fate.
Regret won't fix it; you'd better repent!

grade 9
winter 2016

There Is Still Hope

To my grandma

Our streams cut off, our wells poisoned,
rivers diverted, creeks trampled,
no watercourses left, no drops of rain;
infants crying, mothers ebbing …
should I just give up and run away?
No, I won't despair. I say no to misery
because I still have hope!

Drag my pride in the dust,
tread on and trample my self-worth;
laugh, mock, and trash my dignity—
I won't move or swerve
because I still have hope.

Scatter my family, disperse my people,
tear apart all my goals, hamper my progress;
I won't be devastated nor discouraged
because I still have hope.

Change and alter my wages,
deny me my rightful earnings;
even worse, forbid my voice from being heard—
I won't retreat because I still have so much hope.

Strip me of my clothes, rob me of my garments,
beat and bruise my body and soul—
I will neither weep nor cry
because I still have plenty of hope.

grade 9
summer 2016

Content

I'm proud to be who I am:
my precious heritage;
my meaning-loaded, unique name;

my beautiful dark skin.
Let my height speak out loud—
I won't complain of my weight.

Perfect hair just right for me,
perfect body custom-designed,
a masterpiece in my Maker's hands
(yes, perfect in God's eyes!),

perfect voice utterly irreplicable,
perfect walk moving with rhythm,
orderly thoughts irreversible,
no remarks or critics move me.

Ever content to be who I am,
glad to be who I was created to be
in perfect harmony with the way God made me,

perfectly designed in every way,
I couldn't care less what others think or say.
Content and focused, I will walk my way!

grade 9
spring 2016

Slumbering Nations

I breathe in and I tiptoe about.
Nothing moves; no one exhales.
I see bodies and babies on the ground.
I look for help, but who will answer my calls?
I feel darkness pull over the sky.
I run away, but no one will be at my side.
Where is everybody?
How far have they gone?
"Please," I say, "won't someone come out?"
I then realize that the nations must be sleeping,
snoozing in their beds of nonchalant negligence.
"This is a thing of the Africans," they say,
not realizing the same fate is creeping their way.
If only they'd wake up and see that we're intertwined:
a blood spill here today means terror and death there tomorrow.
They'd better wake up and help stop the bloodshed now!

grade 9
spring 2016

Dedicated to My People

Heartbeat intertwined with the grounds,
the soil is my skin.
What burns the land burns me too.
The water is my tears and my sweat,
all part of me, things you cannot separate.
Interwoven, blended, merged body and soul,
my ears are pressed to the ground, waiting;
my heart beating, perpetually pounding;
my eyes ever looking, urging me to wait for something.

My fingers catch every moment, penning down each event.
This is my country, my base, my home.
You may call me a nationalist, a patriot, or whatever you wish.
I choose to live, work, and build,
use my vigor, energy, and enthusiasm to bring change.
Don't urge me to go out on the streets, yell, and recite slogans,
pushing me to face the gun, offer my life as a price,
a price that is not due.
Because if I do die, then who will listen to the ground?
Who will be left behind to feel the pain and bear the burden?
Who will be there to hear the cries of the destitute
and speak on their behalf?
Because if we all opt to die,
it won't be bravery but sheer cowardice,
for who will take care of what's left behind?
Who will toil on the barren ground
and try to make it produce fruit?

Who will preserve and pass down that rich culture,
tell our story to generations yet to be born?

So choose to live. Don't be eager to die!
If we all choose to die, who will dig the grave?
Who will mourn if we all slip away?
Choose to live, for tomorrow will be a better day.

grade 9
fall 2016

Da Dum

Da dum,
my heart beats for those kids on the streets.

Da dum,
my heart sways when I see flowers withering and trees dying.

Da dum,
my heart shrinks when I hear silent cries of abandoned innocent girls.

Da dum,
my heart throbs for the children who might
not have a world to live in.

Da dum,
my heart beats, sways, shrinks, and throbs, for there is life in it.

But if I could only go beyond emotions and feelings,
move a finger, and engage my feet,
then and only then will I know that I'm human
because I moved to help others.

grade9
winter 2016

Feelings of Emptiness

I feel empty, as no one has a place in my heart,
so I search frantically everywhere
to fill that void in my empty heart.
I tell myself I should amass everything in my reach.
I turn to food; I eat and eat
till I have to puke on someone's feet.
I grab a potato, which I thrust into my coin-filled pocket.
I look for friends, thinking it'd be "the perfect
solution" for filling the void in me.
I spend my time and squander my money.
I laugh out loud to suppress the pain.
I tell jokes to divert attention.

But that hollow hole in me still persists,
so I run to play. Maybe that will take the feelings away.
I swing and skip, I toss and catch.
I pick up some pebbles and shove them near the coins and potatoes.
I gather; I hoard, stockpile, and gobble,
but I still have an empty heart.

So I call it a day and begin to stroll home.
I look at the meadows and flocks.
I force a smile. As I pass by, I wave and say hi.
Nothing I try seems to help me out of my trouble.
I empty my pockets and leave behind everything I collected.

As I let go, new ideas flow into my mind.
I dash up the stairs and kneel down.
With my childlike mouth, I blubber
and ask Jesus to enter my empty heart.
A moment of joy and ecstasy,
indescribable peace, unspeakable calmness:
Jesus takes over his rightful place in my heart.
I step back, reflect, and wonder why I had to roam around
when all I had to do was cry out to my God.
No amount of food, endless activities, uncountable friends
could ever fill that void.
Now, no more emptiness, no more desperation:
all I need to do is reach out to Jesus in prayer.

grade 9
summer 2016

Interrogating the Bible

Question it, go ahead.
Ask why it was written, and how old.
Who is the author, man or God?
What about the demons? Shouldn't He have dealt with them?
You seem wise in your own eyes,
wiser than the Creator of heaven and earth!
"Does He even exist?" you ask mockingly,
"If He does, tell Him to meet me."
You question His righteousness and sovereignty:
Why did He make some rich and others poor?
Why did he make whites wealthy and superior,
while the black race has to suffer and remain inferior?
You and your endless questions!
Now it's my turn to ask you:
why do you question a God "that does not exist"?
You then draw from science and logic;
what you failed to understand is God created science and logic.
He reserves the right to keep or break it!
So don't trouble yourself with questions and comments about Him.
I fear you might have to wait till you get to meet Him face to face.

grade 9
summer 2016

Who Am I?

What defines who I am?
My skin color, or the length of my hair?
I know all that, but who *am* I?
I know I like to eat chicken, and I love to drink milk,
but what really defines who I am?
My love for different shades of orange
alongside every color of the rainbow,
my favorite weather, and my fear of the snow?
I can say all of that about me, but still, who am I?
Does my skin or hair color tell me who I am?
Does it define who I will become?
For I believe my actions count;
it doesn't matter what I favor or savor.
But my words and thoughts count too,
so I will be careful. Wouldn't you?

grade 9
spring 2016

You Love Me Anyway

You call me, but I never respond.
You instruct me, but I never heed.
You guide me, but I never follow,
ever disobeying, ever rebelling.
But You love me anyway!
Defying Your Word, remaining lukewarm,
I inflict pain on your Spirit,
but Your love is stronger than all my sins.
No power can quench the fire of your love.
No one can separate me from your eternal affection—
not the color of my skin, not my race,
my disfigured body, my heavy weight,
ever-shifting moods and ungratefulness,
negative words, unending complaints—
despite it all, You love me anyway.

Undeserving I am, I know. But you still call me your masterpiece,
never ashamed of me and ever caring for me,
carrying me in your arms, speaking comforting words
of unfading love, words of assurance.
Nothing can stop You from loving me, Eternal Love.
Oh, how comforting and encouraging to be in your presence!
Here I come, stumbling, faltering, and tripping.
No matter how many times I trip and fall,
deep inside I know You love me anyways.

grade 9
summer 2016

Just for You, My People

I want to be like John the Baptist
so that I may prepare my people;
wise like Solomon
that I may solve their riddles.
I want to fight like Samson
that I may set them free;
be bold like Deborah
leading the multitude.
I wish to speak like Moses
that I may advocate for them;
acquire knowledge like Daniel
that I may teach them.
I want to be pure like Mary
so I can be a blessing for young and old;
become like Nehemiah
to inspire them to rebuild.
I wish I could be like Joseph
to teach them hard work;
resemble Ruth
not ever to swerve.
Above all I long to show them Jesus—the humble Leader!

grade 9
winter 2016

Judging from Afar

You see hatred;
I feel love.
You see me bullying,
yet I'm encouraging.
You see me as power-hungry,
yet I'm humbling myself.
You see me attacking,
yet I'm supporting.
You see from afar and rush to judge;
if you get closer, you might see better, clearer, purer.
All it takes is a little effort. Just a step closer,
then you can see me better.
Let the chain of judgment drop,
the bondage of prejudice unshackle.
Let bitterness vanish,
misconceptions evaporate.
Stop judging from afar; draw closer to see
that I have love, and that's all of me!

grade 9
winter 2016

Commands or Compromise

"Never, never, never," I say.
"Never will I waiver nor relinquish."
I treasure and uphold Your command,
"Thy will be done." I stand firm to the end.
Your Word is more precious to me than silver or gold.
How can I disobey? How can I defy?
Never will I utter a no to You, my Holy One.
Not one of your Ten will be broken.
People keep saying, "You only live once"
or "There is no fun without menace—
go for it and enjoy it!"
I say there is more to life than mere entertainment.
Life is more precious, loaded with meaning.
I would rather sweat for my calling!
Since life offers no do-overs, and we only live once,
I'd better take no chance, and do things right!

grade 10
spring 2017

Father of Heavenly Lights

Lord, I pray that You give me
a pure heart like Yours,
a heart that shivers and trembles at Your Word.
Father, give me thoughts that are full of wisdom,
peace that lasts for eternity,
and a soul that yearns to worship you.

Never leave me nor forsake me, for I struggle.
Show me the righteous path, or else I might stumble.
Lord, be with me forever; do not let me wither,
for without You, I will be like a withered flower
with no fragrance or beauty to make me special.
Lord, be by my side … even when I try run away from you.

grade 10
winter 2017

Creation or the Creator?

Gazing at the ocean
vibrant with colors,
shall I call it turquoise, blue, or emerald green?
A cool breeze blows gently;
fishes of all sorts show off their fins.

Mazing through the jungle, through gigantic trees,
suspicious wild animals stare endlessly.
Exotic birds chirp and make soothing melodies.

The sandy desert, tranquil and mystic;
mountains erected, posing so majestic,
as the orange sun dances and descends.

Look at the icebergs, the work of a sculptor.
You could go on and on praising, singing, and admiring.
But as exciting and impressive as creation might be,
there can be no true joy without the Creator,
the Source of the universe and countless galaxies,
the One and only God
Who brought all forth with only His Words!

grade 10
winter 2017

Enthusiasm

So eager, so keen,
so zealous, so excited,
equipped to work, armed to build—
if I work hard today, change will come tomorrow.
I draft, I write,
I plan and strategize.
I push myself further.
I grab my school bag, and I'm ready to learn.
I sit in class, pen in hand.
writing pad spread,
passion stirring my heart—passion for my people;
to captivate the mind of the youth, inculcate work ethics;
to impart knowledge, instill passion for their nation,
enlighten them about love, love for their people,
love beyond words, not just waving of flags,
shouting on the streets, reciting slogans.
True love goes beyond; it bends down to work,
to build and cultivate, to clean and sanitize.
Oh, how I long to reach out to my people!
I push and shove, dream and work with all my might
that I might build a home for the wanderer and lost,
a home of justice they will never have to flee,
free of poverty, free of prison, free of torture, free of murder.
Oh, how I long to bring a better tomorrow!

grade 10
summer 2017

Halt, Halt, Halt!

Stop it!
Endless bleedings, bruised bodies and broken bones,
aching hearts, pierced souls, tinted memories …

Stop it!
Confusion, mistrust, distrust and grief—
the rules of our days, never the exception.

Stop it!
Hate, discrimination, and separation
raid our minds and hearts.
Why can't we agree to coexist peacefully?
After all, God made us all equally.

Stop it!
Discontinue the killing!
Halt the bombing!
Bring to rest your discrimination!
Eliminate jailing!
Abolish derogatory terms!

Rise up to stop it before it reaches your doorsteps.
Don't close your eyes, wishing it never existed.
Today you are silently watching the unknowns dying;
tomorrow you will be standing in the row of the vanishing.
You'd better stop it now, before it cuts your source of breath.

grade 10
summer 2017

A Double Face

To my brother Toki
who almost became a victim of police brutality

You storm into my house
with clubs and arms,
stomping over my property.
You say you came for security and safety.
You claim to represent the government.
You pull out a piece of paper you call a warrant
and throw it on my face, slicing the air,
invading my privacy, disturbing my peace.
I question your integrity, doubt your legality.

You seem to me a house with no foundation,
a tree without roots.
You present a stamped piece of paper.
"We are here to arrest your brother.
Bring him out!"
You must be a fool to make this kind of demand,
trying to make me a betrayer like yourself,
daring to ask me to hand over the person who carries my roof.
You must be a bunch of fools, a gang of hooligans.
You begin to yell and bark, threatening to drag my brother out.
I feel a chill running down my spine,
overwhelming horror, a rush of terror,
but I refuse to budge.
I hold my breath and make myself look bulletproof.

I feel the weight of eight sets of eyes staring at me.
I deny his presence and begin to stroll away.
You feel offended, your ego shredded;
you begin to threaten, slurring abusive words,
unmasking your hidden face, revealing your arrogance.
You storm into the house, kicking every door open,
searching every corner, sticking your head in every closet.

A child of the millennium, I begin to record your madness,
holding my clandestine phone to capture the monster you are.
You spot my camera; you rage and grab my phone in fury.
I clench it hard, not willing to let go.
My elbow strikes your chest as I try to place the phone closer to me.
You scream and yell, you threaten to throw me in jail.
Family members cry and plead as you push me out,
"She is only a child, underage, a minor. Please
take the phone and let her go …"
Your true color is unmasked, your beastlike character unveiled;
no sense of compassion, no trace of humanity in you.

Unashamed, you claim you are a policeman, not a thief.
You are there to maintain safety and peace.
How can you proclaim peace while you breathe out violence,
a grand hypocrisy, an age-old fallacy?
Mo matter what you do, I won't kneel down for you.
Don't ever expect me to betray my brother.
I don't keep two faces like you.
You'd better face your deceptive self.
Buy the truth; do not sell it!

grade 10
summer 2017

Saints

To all who came to our rescue

Unlawful men in "lawful" uniforms
invading my safety zone,
raiding our private home,
threatening to capture, torture, and kill,
searching for my brother hidden in the corner
(whole body shaking, knees giving way),
hearts pounding, tears streaming,
family in shambles, hopes dying—
when darkness looms,
Injustice rules.
When sounds make me jolt,
arrogant men sneering and threatening,
who will speak against this injustice?
When my hope is blown out,
who will hear my silent cry?
Who will light up my path?
When my reality shatters and my future evaporates,
when my life comes under threat,
when I despair, fearing it's all going to come to an end,
saints are sent to guide me, angels in the flesh:
ordinary people who fight their own battles
but are willing to share my pain,

ordinary people who are genuinely kind,
companions during trials, rescuers in the storm
dispatched by the King, my saving saints
not to be worshiped but to be loved and honored.

grade 10
summer 2017

The Invincible Me

Shall they push me down and trample over me?
No, they shan't!
Shall they spill my blood and rest?
No, they shan't!
Shall they poison my waters
and watch me wither and blow away?
No, they shan't!
Shall they burn my flesh and toss my ashes in an unmarked grave?
No, they shan't!
Shall they raise a gun and blow my head?
No, they shan't!
For God is on my side
even if they plot and try to capture me,
trapping me in their snares.
No, they shan't!
For He stands with me
and
no wind shall try to knock me down.
No, they shan't!

grade 11
winter 2018

Creation Nonsense

Darwin's evolution, Big Bang's progression
negating the Creator, denying the source of creation,
inculcating young minds is pure indoctrination.

You tell me it's right and a proven fact.
Is that so? But why does nature refute your theory?
The glistening sea speaks of the Creator's glory,
the beauty of the setting sun, the sparkle of stars at night,
all testify to His wonder and might.

Don't you realize it's demeaning to us humans
to say we evolved from an ape?
To view one another as the result of accident?
No, we were made fearfully and wonderfully,
with eternal plans and everlasting existence
In His own image, dignified and honored.

I won't fall for deceptions that humans are apes,
but if you are eager to learn the truth of creation,
Genesis 1:31 is my recommendation;
and if you persist that humans are still evolving,
stars are still crashing, birthing new creation,
Psalm 14, verse 1, will tell you your true position.
And if you insist on digging deeper,
you may stride to Romans 1, verse 22.

grade 11
fall 2018

Tears, Regrets, and Remedies

Tears find their way around
much like streams but without ground.
Memories are displayed; regrets arrayed.
Mistakes committed line up;
words spoken carelessly crop up.

Pain fills the air, remorse that follows people everywhere.
Fear crawls in and instigates pain of the unknown.
Teeth begin to chatter together as the body quivers;
it shivers, but not from the cold—
rather from blunders made in days of old.

Eyes grow and shrink in an instant;
the realization of death hits.
It blows mercilessly hard, not holding anything back.
Unpleasant memories congregating,
thoughts of guilt flocking,
regrets for words once uttered,
words collected now bouncing off the corners of the mind—
ss there no hope to take them back?

No, it is never too late to repent,
never too hard to mend broken relationships.
It only takes a few humble steps,
while uttering simple but genuine words:

"I am sorry for the words I said and the pain I caused."
Tears once again will start to flow—
never tears of regret
but tears of joy for the relationship restored.

grade 11
winter 2018

Walking on Turbulent Waters

To the servant leader I admire

A lonely walk
is the path I take,
a path mapped out before I came to be,
designed in the heavenly realm,
resolved by heavenly council,
a road I must walk.
I must shoulder a burden.
I must sound a voice—
I can't silence nor suppress it.

But you! While you sit in the boat,
all you see is my tie and suit,
a smile I cemented to my face
to hide my pain and all my scars.
You don't see beyond what you hear,
nor will you hear of more than you see:
you simply want to draw an image of me—
just the surface, since you value no depth.

You accuse me of wearing a sheep's skin,
when in reality it is as authentic as it can be,
genuine as a child newly born.
Why can't you understand
I'm doing it all alone,
drinking the bitter cup with an inner groan?

My own brothers betray me,
frustrated family members accusing me.
I have no friends on this walk I'm walking;
no companions accompany me.
But I must do it.
I must march on.
I must fulfill my purpose,
even if I'm all alone.
This is the very essence of what I'm made for:
to let love lead,
to allow mercy to take the seat,
to ensure that justice rolls like a river,
to make the future brighter as I burn and melt down.
Don't say it's a facade I display
nor an "illusion fused with confusion," as you like to say.
I take no aim at political gain
but follow a man who sacrificed every inch of himself
to replace centuries of curse with abundance and prosperity.

On this treacherous and lonely journey, I bounce back and forth,
forgetting "the battle is not mine"—
not at all!
The invisible yet invincible Holy Spirit is on my side.
On this dark and cold journey of mine,
His warmth and love comfort and shield me.
He is the Guarantee that I won't drown.
Determined, unflinching, unwavering,
I will continue to be a sojourner
on the cold turbulent waters
as I reach out to the outstretched arms of the One
who commands the storm and raging waters:
Jesus—the Alpha and Omega of my leadership journey!

grade 12
spring 2019

The Writing on the Wall

The writing on the wall,
so foreign, so far-off,
needs deciphering,
heavy interpretation.

Tell me what it means?
Is it a warning or a plea?
Does it speak of my end?
Will my towers crash down?
Could this be my last night, my last hour?

Could it be some sort of annunciation?
The sound of proclamation
that I may celebrate,
shout for joy, leap and dance?
Could this be announcing the fulfillment of my promise?
Will this mark a new start, the breaking of a new era?
Could it be designating the hour to shout out hooray?

Tell me, wise One, what is the writing on the wall?
Where does this mysterious hand branch from?
What will become of my riches,
wealth accumulated over ages,
of the kingdom I built,
The renown I gained, the fame I acquired?

Tell me, wise One, the fate of my legacy?
Will my history become a mere fallacy?
Will I cease to exist before the morning sun?
Will all my great work be undone?
Don't hide it from me, mystery revealer:
I promise to lavish you with gold and purple,
confer upon you a great power and gifts of royalty,
if only you reveal to me the writing on the wall.

spring 2019

A Divine Kiss

A kiss from heaven,
Lord—blow a divine kiss towards me.
Hold me in Your embrace and tell me that You love me.
Reassure me that Your promises are true.
Sooth me with Your words and confirm to me that I'm still Yours.

Sins of the past echo in my mind.
My inequities and trespasses resonate.
My accuser kindles and rekindles memories of old,
but Lord, I know one divine kiss will restore my soul.

Even if I rolled in the mud after You'd dressed me in white,
Lord, kiss me. Even if my mouth still spews out salt and brine,
may Your divine kiss bring me comfort and tranquility.
Your everlasting love is my sanctuary and serenity
Kiss me, Father, to repair my tattered heart—
A divine kiss undoubtedly will soften my hardened heart.

spring 2019

Visible Love

Lord, I want my love for You to be visible,
visible like paint on the painter's canvas,
Vibrant colors splattered and splashed on my clothes and hair.

Lord, I want people to spot it from afar;
I want it to be as tall and as visible as the cedar of Lebanon,
as bright as the constellation of stars in the darkest of nights.

Lord, I want my love for You to be as noticeable as a choir girl's voice
ringing and sounding in all the hallways I cross.

Lord, I want my love for You to pervade and
permeate my surrounding air.
May it be an overflowing aroma which invades the atmosphere.

Lord, I want Your love to elate and intoxicate me,
to uplift my soul and take me to indescribable heights.
I would climb any mountain to make my love for You visible,
as visible as the banner of victory planted on the summit.
Lord, please be my identity, my sole proprietor;
make me a vessel to display Your glory and splendor.

summer 2019

Beautifying Worship

Lord, breathe a new spirit into my heart
that I may worship You in truth and spirit,
a true worship that might captivate You;
beautifying worship, an aroma pleasing to You.

Give me Your promise to turn my fire blue,
a heavenly fire that refines me and makes me pure as gold
to shape and mold me in the image of Your Son.
Calm my ever turning and tossing emotions;
let my flesh die and my spirit regain control.

Let steadfastness and resoluteness be my hallmark.
Anoint my lips to proclaim that your kingdom comes.
Make me a true worshipper, a sabbath of Your rest.

May my voice rings chants of the saints.
Along with Your mighty angels, let me praise and worship You
with an undivided heart and with my whole might
as I submit and surrender my whole being to You.

Lord, what can be as beautiful and as pleasing in Your sight
as a sacrifice of broken spirit and a repentant heart,
the meekness and humility of Your Son Jesus Christ?
May His beauty impart on me that kind and gentle heart.

summer 2019

The Dancing King

What if David was uncoordinated?
What if he moved with passion and no rhythm?
What if people snickered on the sidelines
As he spun in circles, dancing before the Ark of the Covenant?
What if David moved in jerky moves?
What if he cried and laughed but wasn't pleasing to look at?
What if the girls were not there to celebrate
him with their tambourines?
What if the whole procession looked awkward and ungainly?

Shouldn't a king have kept his dignity?

What if everyone stopped looking?
What if only one set of eyes were laid on him,
the eyes that belonged to the Holiest of holies?

What if he praised and danced on the
streets as he did in his chamber?
What if he moved and sang only with the Lord in mind?
What if he worshiped with his whole strength and might?
What if he only saw God before him?

If that is the case, I want to be just like David;
not David, His Majesty,
but David worshiping in humility and honesty.

fall 2019

99

Mercy and Hope

There's still hope.
I crossed the sea,
climbed over the mountains.
I ran and ran
farther than I have ever before.
I drowned myself in sin,
chained myself with pain.
Guilt was my bondage;
lies and fabrications became my propeller.

I went far, and far
off I went;
no way to return,
no road left to trace.

I saw it all, nothing left:
addictions and anger,
one blunder followed by another.
I became riddled with shame,
but I didn't know how to reverse it,
nor did I know the way to forgiveness,
drenched in self-pity and remorse.

There was no one to blame but me,
no one to help as I drifted away.
But I cried out anyway.

I somehow caught a little glimpse of hope,
a sparkle in the dark,
a whisper to my heart:
"Do not fear, my child.
I'll take you to a place where mercy and hope abound."

fall 2019

Despotes

Your strength is boundless; they call you Omnipotent.
The speed of light does not compare with Your swiftness.
You cannot be defined nor contained, for you are omnipresent.
I stand before You in awe; in holy fear I tremble and shudder.

Unimaginably, immeasurably, You are great and infinite
but You stoop low to save the weak and the fatherless,
destitute children who have no one to love.
I know you are the One, the One who calls
Himself Father to the fatherless,
Despotes!

You fight on behalf of the defenseless.
You shut the mouth of the roaring lion.
A listener to the groans of the prisoners,
You speak on behalf of the voiceless.
Despotes!

I know you are the complete authority.
The sun and moon submit to You.
Mountains leap in Your presence;
Oceans rise and fall at Your glance.
I know who you are: You are the *Despotes*!

Lord, I pray that creation acknowledges
That You are the Cause of boundless resources.
The whole of creation is in Your arsenal.

The hearts of kings are channeled by Your command
Like streams of water diverted by Your Word.

Show them that You wield the largest army.
Multitudes of angels and saints await your order.
Let the mouth of Your archangel start a war cry!

No armament, no weapon can keep You bound,
for You yield unrestricted power,
never limited and always around.
Show them that You are the boss from that small little town.

fall 2019

Asking for a Sign

I need a sign Lord, a sign that You're with me,
a token that I can hold on to.
I don't need anything grand or heavy,
nor am I asking for the extraordinary or even savvy.

I won't ask for gold or silver.
I care not for sapphire or emerald.
Lord, I'm so modest, only asking for the simplest,
as simple as a small rock.

A rock?
I heard that a little rock brought a giant to his knees.
I read that from a rock You gushed out water in the wilderness.
You split a rock when Moses sought a hiding place
and caused rocks to crumble in Jericho with a simple shout.
Lord, I'm so modest, only asking for the simplest.

A well?
If You would only open my eyes and show me the well,
I could use my own spring like mother Hagar,
or if you'd let me reopen the ancient wells like Isaac,
I wouldn't fear disputers like Sitnah nor Esek.
Lord, I'm so modest, only asking for the simplest.

Rain?
Lord, if You'd drench my fleece wet
while leaving the ground dry as you did for Gideon,
or if You poured the rain in the driest season,
I promise not to anger you by trading You for a human king.
Lord, I'm so modest, only asking for the simplest.

Lord, I'm not asking for much,
just a small sign to encourage me on my walk,
just between You, me, and the angels.
It doesn't have to be public;
others don't need to know.
Just command a miracle so that I too can go with Your flow.
Lord, I'm so modest, only asking for the simplest.

winter 2019

Find Me

Lord, find me.

Find me in my brokenness,
bare and naked,
exposed and ashamed.
Cover me with Your grace.

Lord, find me in my deceitfulness,
soaked in trickery and dishonesty.
May Your truth heal me and make me upright.

Lord, find me in my grief and sorrow,
hopeless and despairing as I worry about tomorrow.
Anoint me with Your oil of joy.

Lord, find me in my rage and anger
as I yell and scream at heaven and earth.
Whisper into my heart Your calming words.

Lord, find me in my worries,
soaked in anxiety, terror, and panic.
Breathe into me transcending peace.

Lord, find me at my worst.
Catch me unprepared,
unclean, and in my mess.
Speak order into my life.

For I do not fear You seeing me at my lowest.
I won't hide from You my failure and my defeat.
You still love me, even when I'm weary and weak.

winter 2019

My Hidden Sin

Hidden sin, stolen fruit I savor in secret—
my little fingers, so greedy, so tricky,
latching on to what's hidden,
clenching deadly sinful practices—

crush the evil behind those little fingers.
Break deep, entrenched wickedness buried in my bones.
Nip it in the bud that it may never grow.

My red heart, so evil, so twisted,
pumping life into dead sin,
revitalizing evil thoughts meant to be gone,

stab it! Ravage and tear it into pieces.
Wreck its muscles, render it no use.
Tear it and destroy it before it takes my soul.

My complicated mind, so envious, so torturous,
opening doors meant to be closed,
Threading together memories that should be kept apart,

smother it, strangle it!
Tear it apart, destroy it, let it vanish
That I may not be thrown out.

Father, You know my hidden sins,
concealed and buried deep in my innermost being.
No sin is hidden from You:
You see it crouching, desiring to have me.
Awaken me, empower me that I may rule over it.

winter 2020

Congratulations

Straighten what I have bent.
Mend what I have shattered.
Heal what I have wounded.
Awaken what's in deep slumber.

Doctor,
I know you have all the answers.
Forgive me for my sickly composure.
Medicate my hollow behavior.

Abba, Father,
put me to sleep and remove practices hidden under.
Operate on my thoughts and yearnings.
Stitch together my tongue, for it utters unholy words.

Nurse,
rock me to sleep that I may find rest.
Hold me gently that I may feel the warmth of Your embrace.
Tell me I did well and that my fight is almost over.

"Congratulations!"
I hear from the heavenly corridors.
"Welcome home, you brave and mighty soldier.
Race completed, victory won; welcome to your eternal home!"

spring 2020

Concealed in His Quiver

A secret weapon,
concealed from the enemy's eyes
keep me in your quiver.

Let me be one of your chosen weapons,
An arrow You use to rout Your enemies.

Make me swift and dangerous.
Let me breach the enemy's territory.

Father, keep me in your shadows.
Under Your wings I'll always remain invisible.

Reveal to me how You predestined me,
plans You had for me before the universe came to be,
prophetic utterances given while I was in my mother's womb
That I may fulfill Your eternal purpose.

Master, let me be Your secret weapon,
a mighty war club for a time of combat,
a fierce sword for the day of battle.
Please put me to full use that I may destroy powers of darkness.

spring 2020

Abba

"Father, Jesus, Lord!" I cried.
In the blink of an eye, You responded.
You said, "Call unto Me, I will answer thee
And show thee great and mighty things."

You rescued me from a bottomless pit.
In the blink of an eye, You responded.
You lifted me with an outstretched arm.
You hid me under the shadow of Your wings.

From a road traveled far and distant
To your holy presence where I find delight,
From the land of agony and self-inflicted abomination,
I cried out to You to rescue me.
In the blink of an eye, You responded.

You say I am never too far gone.
You can always hear my voice from the farthest horizon.
In the blink of an eye, You responded.
Now I dare to call You Abba, Father.
You allowed me to recline at Your table.
Your amazing grace welcomed me home.

spring 2020

Handpicked

I reach for you,
A daughter's hand outstretched to hold her father's.
I reach for you,
anticipating warmth which will seep into my cold fingers.
"Do not fear," You whisper into my ear.
I've put my trust in You, I have no worries.

You handpicked me to serve You. I know You set me apart.
The grip of Your love subdued my rebellious heart.
In Your presence I know no fear.
I gain strength gazing into Your warm fiery eyes.
Even if a battalion marches out against me,
I will not lose faith, for You are on my side.

Covered by Your blood I shall slay the Dragon.
Like a mighty warrior, You ravage my enemies.
As I am Your little lamb, You hoist me on your shoulders,
shoulders higher than any demon can climb.
Inexpressible, immeasurable is Your love,
Demonstrated in the sacrifice of Your only Son.
You sent Him down under the ground
That I might be seated next to Your righteous right hand
Above in the heavens and galaxies full of stars.

summer 2020

God's Friend

Lord, find a friend in me.
Confide in me as You did little Samuel.
Let me be the one you rest your head on,
a friend You pour out Your heart to,
the one you call in the dead of night.

Say to me what You said to Abraham:
"My servant, my chosen, my seed."
Assure me that You will not hide any measures You plan to take.

Lord, let me wrestle with you like Jacob.
Make me a true friend who cleaves at all times,
One who sticks by you even when people think we're fighting.

Lord, let me be a friend you call again and again.
Call me with a sweet nickname as You called Jedidiah.
Vow to me that You will always keep me in Your presence.

Let me share in Your sufferings. Make me sip from that bitter cup.
Allow me to dress Your wounds that family and friends inflicted.
Let me be a friend who accompanies you on your long journeys.
Find a friend in me, for I found a true Friend in you.

summer 2020

Sennachrib

Yes, I am boisterous and unruly.
My pride has surpassed the stars high in the sky.
I raise my voice; my threats echo past the guards.
Humanity trembles as I recount past achievements and triumphs.
I slur blasphemous words: "Can your God
save out of my mighty hands?"

This is my moment to shine, a moment to
prove I am one amongst the gods.
With my countless chariots and charioteers,
I will ascend high to heavens.

As I brawl and broil, I fall asleep and dream
of how I'd wake up to fight.
I raise war shouts as I march down to camp.
I'm still in a dream—no, a night mare, I say
as I gaze on dead bodies of my whole army.
One angel of God smiting one-hundred eighty-five thousand?
I flee back home like a fish with a hook in its mouth.
Little did I know against whom I raised my voice.

I can't retaliate, for I was defeated in the dead of the night.
Like grass I withered and was tossed away to be burnt.

I, King Sennachrib, lost my power and might,
no longer feared and respected for I touched the Untouchable.
I should have listened when they said lack of wisdom kills the fool.
If only I had sold all I owned and bought wisdom!

summer 2020

Inertia

From a deep slumber I awaken.
I don't want to depart from the comfort of my bed.
I don't want to leave the ease I feel.

My mornings are dark and gloomy.
The chill outside my window seems to be wrestling.
The worries for the day hound me.
Lord, be gracious to me.

My body refuses to move.
My eyes shut in fear of the unknown.
My heart lulls me back to sleep.
"Why worry?" says a voice.
"Why move? Why resist?
Opt for ease; choose tranquility instead.
Just roll over and pull the covers closer.
There is no need to awaken."

My ears join in,
Sounds start to fade,
tugging me back to bed,
making me numb to everything
outside the windowpane.
"Sleep," they say. "Slumber,
waste away your day."

I try to fight it.
I try to move, but my flesh seems to get its way.
"Wake up, wake up," I say.
"Wake up! You have a lot to do today."

"Lord," I cry out,
"my salvation in times of distress!
Do you see me? Lord, please save me.
I don't want to sleep my life away!
I don't want to waste this precious gift of time.
I must try to bring even if it is a small change.
Lord, be my strength, and let me defeat this drowsiness,
however lulling and soothing it might seem."
I choose to resist it; I refuse to be shackled.
I command the chains holding me down to fall off,
away from my purpose, away from life filled with grace.
In Jesus's glorious name,
I will rise to conquer my whole entire day!

summer 2020

Call Me by Name

My body feels numb,
yet my fingers are trembling.
I'm stiff and sweaty,
yet my mind is dancing.

My tongue breaks free;
it is pushing the boundaries.
I have so much to say,
nut I'm slowly wasting,
wasting the time I have.
Emotions piled deep inside,
I want to fly away, but I fear I might land,
land from this high I'm feeling,
one that I can't quantify in time.
I fear my embrace won't hold us together long enough.

I look for hope as I slowly perish.
I know You will come in and rescue me
before I completely ebb away.

I see Your big hands swoop low
and swing me into Your embrace.
I find a cleansing water to wash my sins away.

I wanted to escape, vanish with the wind.
But Your love took a hold of me,
My Creator and Savior who calls me by name.

summer 2020

Prince of Peace

Peace against the darkness that looms ahead,
war against the evil within;
tranquility rooted down in the heart,
zeal at the epicenter of the gut—

Peace!

Peace on the terrors awaiting at every corner,
war on the snares ahead of running feet;
wisdom on the nails of the fingers
Unfathomably deep and visible within—

Peace!

Peace is knocking at the door. Will someone let him in?

Crown on his head,
robe reaching down to his feet,
golden sash around his chest,
sword ready despite the victory he already won,

he beckons us to
come fight the good fight.

winter 2020

Eternal Victor

Do not fear.
Do not lose courage
for the battle is already won.
You have to faithfully march on!

Rejoice!
You are under the headship of that Mighty Warrior,
the Marshal of the heavenly host.
Rejoice!
For He is not only the Commander
but also the Divine Orchestrator.

If the enemy is defeated and victory is already won,
why are havoc, chaos, and confusion immensely rampant?
Well, if you take time to inquire and investigate the nature of war,
you will discover that you're experiencing only an aftermath.

Now, I advise you to learn how to live like a victor.
Stop seeing yourself as a mere victim.
Remember that you are more than a conqueror
through the One who was revealed to destroy the work of the Devil:

Jesus, the Champion of eternity!

Winter 2020